Dark Sky Park

For everybody, of all ages, in the groups from which these poems
grew... and for Rose, who realised that good science is as beautiful
as art – P.G.

With love to my parents, Fanny and Ben – J.H.

With thanks to the friendly e
of Wales in Cardiff, where Pl
face to face.

Text copyright © Philip Gross 2018

Illustrations copyright © Jesse Hodgson 2018

First published in Great Britain in 2018 by
Otter-Barry Books, Little Orchard, Burley Gate,
Herefordshire, HR1 3QS
www.otterbarrybooks.com

ISBN 978-1-910959-88-6

Illustrated with brush and ink

Set in Warnock Pro

Printed in the United Kingdom

9 8 7 6 5 4 3 2 1

Dark Sky Park

Poems from the Edge of Nature

PHILIP GROSS

Illustrated by
JESSE HODGSON

Otter-Barry BOOKS

CONTENTS

Night Walker

There is a place (believe me,
    she said) where if, if
      you go beyond
the street lights, to the lane's end,
    then (and don't look back)
      walk on...

(One flash could nix your night-sight,
    the spark of a car on the hill
      a mile away
or a patio light's twitchy sensor
    shocking empty gardens
      with fake day.)

Just walk, she told me once. You'll see
    what owl-eyes, fox-eyes, know:
      there is a place
behind the darkness. It's like coming home,
    she said, believe me. I hope
      it was true.

Look up. The height of it! More stars
than anyone has seen. And one
small speck called you
among the millions. And you're spinning
upwards (she said, the last time
we saw her) through

the brilliant dark, the depth, of space.

*Many animals have better night vision than we have. It takes
about five minutes in the dark for our eyes to adapt and pick up
faint light.*

Life on the Ledge

The world goes straight up,
straight down, mostly.
Nothing else keeps still,

not the sky, not the sea.
Only the cool grey granite
holds us, like a mother,

though the ledge

is growing smaller day by day.
I think we are too many
and the more we eat

(we have to – we scream
at the sky – it feeds us
through our parents' beaks)

the closer to the edge...

Stiff tufts of sea-pink
tremble in the wind.
We sit tight. Far below

the sea is growling
and grinding its teeth,
impatient. In the gusts

even the unhatched egg

rocks on its bare shelf.
The air is no-go, no shape
but it tugs at us,

ruffles our feathers, gets
inside them like an itch
we have to scratch

with a quiver, a stretch

of the wings. First,
a hop and a teeter – *no!*
shrink back and huddle

till the day a new wind
whispers *Now!*
Fly! And (we have no say

in this) our wings answer *Yes!*

*One of the smaller kinds of gull, kittiwakes nest on narrow
ledges on vertical cliffs. Chicks are born with an instinct to
keep very still.*

Black Smokers

And here, where light can't reach, where sound can't stir
    in water that would grip
        you and squeeze, like a grape
in its fist... Here, in the deepest you can think... the earth

confides her secrets, just a crack. Where continental plates
    tear very slowly down the seam,
        her dark gifts bloom
in sulphur smoke that boils up from crags, from stalagmites

like dripping candles growing upwards, the reverse
    of burning down. Here, down
        is up. And clustered round
the vent like one lit window, lightless lives are clustering

to warm themselves, to gaze in at the furnace door
    where life itself is being forged.
            Think of an adoration
in a manger. Imagine all the homeless, all the poor,

are summoned to the feast. Think. Close your eyes.
    This might be where
            we came from, before
anything. Do you remember, deep down, deep inside?

*A black smoker is an opening in the deep sea bed where water
gushes out from the earth's crust, heated to temperatures much
hotter than boiling by the molten rock below. The minerals
dissolved in it form black clouds that settle out to form 'chimneys'
as much as 60 metres high.*

Tardigrade Saga (1)

There are more than 1,000 species of tardigrades, Short, plump, eight-legged, they are also known as water bears or moss piglets.

The largest are only half a millimetre long. They have been on earth for 500 million years, and can live in the most extreme environments.

Their tactic is to dry their bodies out to a tiny hard capsule. Like this, they have been known to survive even in the vacuum of deep space.

Tardigrade in Transit

Pack me up in a plain brown wrapper
of myself
        and post me to the future.
(Hey, me! Happy birthday, whenever we are.)

Leave everything I don't need on the journey
at the airport,
        all my food and water. Ship me
as a flat-pack kit, with the instructions in my genes.

Puzzle over them later, when you gaze into
the microscope.
        You'll see me, back from frozen,
from deep space or from deep ocean...
           can it be...? Yes, look,
               I'm waving back at you.

*

Tardigrade in Long Shot

Zoom in
to deep moss forest
as lush as the Amazon
in any damp corner of any back yard.

Adjust the lens
× 2, × 8, × 32 ...
You're falling out of the sky
towards it like a pilot baled out
from a supersonic flight. Your parachute

      fills out with light,

like a blown seed drifting down, down
(even gravity can take its time
here) – in to a place
without names.

The green world opens up its arms
(zoom one click more) to catch
you, to gather you in.
Welcome home.

*

Tardigrade in its Element

This is the kingdom of the Water Bear.
To enter here, you have to shrink
and slow down, down. A day
is one tick of the clock, one blink

of the sun's eye. Overhead, like tangling
mangrove, see the stiff moss-trunks,
the flutes of fruiting lichen with its scarlet
cups of spores... You have to think

like an explorer – no, like a guest
of this generous jungle, with its globes
of dew, its swamp pools where who knows
what creatures may come down to drink.

If someone was to speak now,
back in the high and mighty world,
the lost world you belonged in,
it would be thunder, huge and indistinct,

just a rumble and quake. The glistening
water quivers. Settles slowly. Or not. There,
look: something's moving in the shadows
spilled across the forest floor like ink,

something huge, and in its element:
the great Moss Pig, the Water Bear.

First Plant on Dry Land

There is always a first. Just the one.
For time and time and time

there was ocean, going soupy with the slop
and gloop of life.

Somewhere else, great boilerplates of rock,
parched by sun,

scrubbed by wind, no mercy – that was land.
What rain came

boiled straight off it, hissing in a fit of steam.

*

What sense did it make, to step into the open,
shuffling out of the cool, the all-providing sea,
leaving home?

Don't you believe them if they say there was a plan.
This wasn't a beach-head. I was beached.
High and dry.

One moment in a tide pool, then… a glistening salt pan,
in shivering heat, in the withering scorn
of the sky.

This was a whole other planet, though it was
    the same one.

*

I held on, till sunset.
In the dark came a flat-tasting dew,
just enough. Then day happened again.

These were the odds.
No, there wasn't a plan. All you need
is the first, some loner, dope or dupe or holy fool.

What no one could know
was half the life back in the sea-trench
would watch me go over the top, exchange a glance,

and shrug (a slow one,
the odd million years), then take
a breath, and follow. (There are some down there,

deep thinkers, who say all this was one big mistake.)

*Plant life, like all life, started in the oceans. The first,
like low-growing moss or lichen, appeared on land about
450 million years ago.*

Snow Leopard

... not white like the snow,

more moon-panther or silvery cloud-cat
with her ripple-patterns melting as (oh,

but she's beautiful) you stare
while valley mist whirls up and blows

between the boulders, or the sun breaks through
and all the edges are a smattering of shadows,

a glint on wet rock. Now she's still,
crouched. Now... sprung. There she goes

ledge to ledge, bound by bound,
as stones go rattling to the scree below

and wild goats scatter. She has one
marked. That one. (Play the chase scene slow

as films do, as if this might be for ever,
these last moments the poor prey will know.)

But it's off, the scraggy old big-bottomed
tahr – stumbling, you'd think, falling – no,

think again, as with rubbery fantastic
poise it leaps (there is a half mile drop below)

and catches itself, teeters like a tightrope
clown... leaps, snatching inch-wide footholds

with clattery hooves, down – leaving leopard
stranded, panting, stumped. Why are we so

in love with beauty, with its claws and teeth,
as though this is *its* story, not our own

and the goat's – that plucky comedy
played out through centuries

between the sheer drop and the killing snow?

*The snow leopard is a rare big cat found in the highest
mountain ranges of Asia. There may be only a few
thousand of them left in the wild.*

*The Himalayan Tahr is a tough and agile wild goat.
It lives on almost sheer rocky mountainsides and is
the snow leopard's main prey.*

from the Extreme Sports Olympics:

Lava~Boarding

It's a long climb to the crater's lip.
    Peek over, gape and gag
at the smeech of sulphur, the drop

to black scree, funnelled inwards
        to the pit

that breathes... bloop, a yellowish
    burp of steam, fire-lit
from under by a pulsing glow.

Now you see it, in its black crust
      like a heavy overcoat,

the liquid fire – live lava fidgeting
      about to rise. You're ready
for it, waiting – you have all the kit.

You could wait all day, all night. But
      now, this is it,

yes, the beautiful disaster you've come
    halfway round the world
to meet. It coughs, spews, and you run

to where the fissure opens – the first
    sizzling tongue

of the eruption. Dry thorn bushes
    leap into sparks at its touch
and you're fumbling: your asbestos

suit, your fireman's helmet with black
    tinted glass,

the foot-thick lava-board. Now – wait
   for it... you jump
with spaceman slowness. You're upright

in an updraught that's trying to wrestle
   you right off your feet

and riding it, cresting it, like the dire
   god the ancients spoke of
who held all the earth's anger inside

till he came riding down the mountain
   on his chariot of fire.

There are real extreme sports such as white-water rafting and bungee jumping, but we can always imagine more. Please don't try this at home.

Arctic Terns

Towards the Point, there's no
      more that a tree can do
except to crouch low – just a few
scrub oaks, a stunted willow

then there's nothing but lichen
      at home on the stones
– or here and there an inch-high
yellow flower that's here and gone

between tides. The boulders
      huddle close into each other's
shelter, tight against the cold
as the stone-spit narrows, and the weather

grips you, and the emptiness.
      Then, at the last
rock, when you think there can't be less
of everything, this! Falling out of the vast

North sky, all clash
      and clamour, shriek and wheel
like knife grinders in flight (the rush
of their wings is the whetstone and steel):

sea-swallows, Arctic Terns
      like cold flames, like the sun's

white shadows, like a crown of thorns
at our heads... At our feet, among the stones,

their nests... It is suddenly clear:
        this emptiness is full
and we're the one thing too much here
as we turn and trip and stumble,

quick, before the tide turns on us too.

It's nothing personal. Go home.

*Known as sea swallows because of their grace in the
air, Arctic Terns will attack anything that comes too
near their nests among the stones.*

Aleppo Cat

First, months
of flash, thud, shudder,

then the wailing...
Months,
that's half a young cat's life

and three or four more of her nine
already used up.
Hush,

ears perked, head cocked,
she's listening
to the sound

that's no sound, no voice, not
a throb of engines, not one
sound of human.
Now

she slinks, always liquid enough
to shrink through cracks,
now starved to whisker-thinness

– pauses,
wide eyes
between tumbled blocks,

the first living thing out
among the heaps of mudbrick
dust, of a...
           who could say

street? She checks the cat-map
in her mind. The market...
Where the bread smells came from...
Gone.
           And where the fish man
tossed the bones.
                       Gone.

Where the children chased her
with fierce cuddles, too young
to know their strength.
                       Gone,
and their voices,

           out late, playing,
their mothers calling them home.
Home, gone. Aleppo,
           gone, gone, gone.

*When this was written, the city of Aleppo in Syria was under
siege, being destroyed by both sides in a civil war. There will be
other cities, other wars.*

The Toughest Thing You Never Noticed

... until now: Ivy-Leaved Toadflax,
   you know, that trickle of pale mauve,
poached-egg yellow and white
like spilled paint on a bare stone wall

   but moving – dipping,
   bobbing and reaching in the wind,
at home here standing, dancing even,
a toehold on nothing at all,

   no earth, no ledge, no hope,
   you'd think... except look:
these fuse-wire tendril-tips,
these fine root hairs of mine,

   they're like brilliant questions
   put to governments or bullies
in a whisper: no force, just a *Why?*
and a *Why?* and a *Why*

   Not? in the right place
   at the right time, in the slightest
hairline crack. I've a smidgen
of dust and a raindrop to drink

   and that's plenty. Look close
   at my un-pretty pert pug faces

in their own crowd, grinning. Grow
is what we do instead of think:

try this, try that, swaying, hey,
in the whatever breeze. Call me
Wandering Sailor, Mother of Thousands;
in French, call me *Ruine-de-Rome*.

I'm here, I'm everywhere
you never look. On the brink,
on the edge, with no visible means
of support... but at home.

*A tough little climber with pretty mauve flowers, this
plant has spread from the Mediterranean area around
the world. It goes by many names.*

*Brought over in the cracks of Roman statues, it's been
at home in Britain for 400 years. You find it growing on
stone walls almost anywhere.*

A Tardigrade By Any Other Name

You say *tardigrade* – slow-stepper,
sluggish walker, micro-sloth. Or,
if you want to get familiar, *water bear*.
Moss-piglet, if you must. Compare
me to a hangdog flannel on a hook,
a rucked-up carpet, a rumpled settee
on the move, or my lips to a rusty bit
out of your parents' tool kit. Call me
slump-slug, bumble-bug or mighty
mould-mite, speck of dust...
                              Or let's
                  get scientific,
                  get specific:
Trogloarctus (that means 'cave bear')
Coronarctus verrucatus ('warty crowned bear' – no
    thanks)
Florarctus pulcher ('pretty flower-bear' – I could live
    with that)

And so on. Throw the book
at me, and have you got me? Truly? Look
into the mirror. Look into your eyes. Look deep,
    look far.

Say each and every name
that you've ever been called.

Now, does that tell you who you are?

*

Tardigrade in Historical Costume

See this now:
the steep red roofs of Delft. The year is 1702
     and the summer is weary.
In the Lowlands, long weeks without rain,

and Master Anton van Leeuwenhoek
who has spent half his seventy years
peering through a polished lens at things
     nobody in the room can see

blinks. It must be the dust
blown through the open window. No,
     he looks again. Among the grey
grit scraped from the gutter yesterday

and mixed with water, something
stirs. Out of the dust, the dead dry matter
(hand me a stronger magnifying glass,
     lean closer, do not breathe)

one speck quivers. Puts out stumps
of legs. Picks up the lumpy rucksack of itself
     and walks. Mijnheer van Leeuwenhoek
is reaching for his inkhorn. They must know

of this in London. He will write a letter:
"Dear sirs, Of certain *animalcules*
found in gutters on the roofs... " He will not,
          he knows already, be believed.

Why would they? There is no name
for this yet. He has been at the creation
          of a (very, very small but
still, it would be blasphemy to say it) world.

Anton van Leeuwenboek was the son of a Dutch
basket maker. Working in the cloth trade and with little
formal education, he taught himself how to grind glass lenses
and invented the most powerful microscope of his time,
opening the eyes of the world to the tiniest known organisms.

Tardigrade in Focus

OK, so *you* imagine it: something
a thousand times your size –

a medium village, maybe, or a cloud
with an enquiring mind –

stops... Bends down very close...
Gets out its magnifying glass

and looks at *you*.

Worm Dreaming

mud worm   blood worm
flood worm borne on waters boiling
   liver fluke and tape worm
and the maggot and the leech
   wire worm   fire worm
dire wyrm and dragon coiling
   rag worm and lugworm
making pockmarks on the beach

      worm dreaming
     dreaming many dreams
        a dream for each

spoon worms scale worms
which-end's-the-head-or-tail worms
   shovelhead and paddle
worms with fibre-optic frills
   deep-sea-bed worms
Rasta-headed dread-worms
   sulphur salt and ice worms
who almost nothing kills

      worm dreaming
     worm dreams older
       than the hills

fan worms almost-man-sized worms
here-since-the-land-began worms
　　the worms who built the earth
and the worms who sweep the sea
　　age-old-friend worms
faithful-to-the-end worms
　　humble never-grumble worms
worms who work for free

worm dreaming
dreaming root and branch
and whale and ant
and dinosaur and

dreaming
you and me

Never think that 'worm' means only earthworms.
A huge number of species live in the deep ocean, on land –
sometimes inside other creatures.

None of the worms here, and few of the names, are made
up – apart from (maybe) dragons. In the Old English
language they were called wyrms.

Young Scientist

Just a jam jar of pond water
      held up to the light,
a jar of nothing,
        wasn't it?
But no,

look closer... Now
      a twitch,
almost too small to see
      but bright
as ketchup: bloodworm!

If a biro scratch
      in red
could have scribbled itself
      in water,
then tried to escape,

or if it could tie
      a quick double clove hitch
in itself, pull it tight
      like elastic, flick loose
just to tangle again...

He thought of long hours
        in the long grass
lazing, gazing straight up at the sky
        on endless
sports days afternoons

nothing to do
        but watch
the see-through specks
        of next to nothing
in his eye –

how they'd twitch
        when he blinked,
then drift
        (the way thoughts do)
against the cloudless blue

like the pond life of heaven,
        like the larval form of angels
at the see-through stage,
        before their wings.
They must be looking down,

he thought, like he was now
        on his jarful of water.
So that was the trick,
        to let your eyes rest half way,
neither here nor there,

to catch the fuse-wire-thin
        red thread,
the almost invisible flick
        of a bloodworm. And
(the way thoughts drift)

he thought of evenings
        past his bedtime
noticing the tiny red veins
        in the corners of his mother's eyes
as she looked up from sewing.

He thought of her sigh.
        He thought,
no, he knew:
        when I'm older,
I really should study these things.

Bloodworms are not worms, but the larvae hatched from eggs that midges lay in water. They are bright red and just visible to the naked eye.

Glacier Worm

Mesenchytraeus solifugus

There is a black canyon
that no one has seen,

a mile deep,
its sides worn smoother by the year

(believe me)
and blackwater rapids, caverns,

boulders tumble-ground to grit
by centuries...

(Close your eyes, and see me.)

> *You think you are dreaming?*
> *No, this is the dream of the ice*
> *that dreams the valley*
> *that dreams me.*

Here, it's the night of all nights,
the deepest darkness,

the leaking away
of cracks of blue-black light

where I go
flinching out of the least touch of sun

which would melt me.
(Your skin would burn and blister

in this cold.)

>*You don't remember?*
>*This is the memory of ice*
>*   that once was everything*
>*   and once again will be.*

Imagine, if you must,
transparent ice fish

thrashing upstream
through the glacier, slower

than you can think.
Imagine snow eagles circling

stately as the moon.
Imagine me (and this

is true) stretched up to drink

where the meltwater seeps,
to pick one grain of pollen

blown from nowhere.
Everything I know

is one drip at a time.
You think that you

can understand this,
living in the blink

between ice ages? No,

you can't imagine.
This is the knowledge of ice,
too deep, too wide, too slow.
    But if you want to try
     to know its mind
      then stop.
      Look close.
      Listen to me.

Mesenchytraeus solifugus is a worm that feeds on pollen and algae in the ice of glaciers. It would die if it became as warm as your fridge.

from The Extreme Music Festival

1. The Storm Harp

Tune up the mountain to the pitch
of music. Set each grass blade quivering.
      Turn up the wind
until the hillside shudders like an animal
shrugging its pelt to scratch an itch.

Hear its sigh. Bring on the bad maraccas
of the slipping scree. The landslide starts.
      Shiver the silver
cymbals of the tarns until they spill;
the glass harmonica of water shatters,

scattering itself in splinters everywhere.
The pressure tightens, tightens, a top string
      that snaps
at the height of a wild cadenza, steel
tip lashing: lightning! Thundrums punch the air.

And through it all, beneath it, hear the slow
harmonics of the choir of cables, thrumming
          between pylons: the great
storm harp, crackling with voltage, that we built
as if for this. Lights dim and flicker in the town below.

Out of the weather we come. Into weather we go.

2. Moon Music

It was always *too much*,
music – always
pummelling her ear drums.
Such air-quakes...

She listened more and more
to less – the final fading
of the violin beyond
its top string, lifting
lark song into space.

She trained her ear to hear,
when even these
disturbances fell still,
the frequencies of light,

the quiver of its wavelengths.
When the sun came out
it was a blare, a brassy fanfare.
Too too much.
She longed for night.

Now she sits with heavy
curtains open just a chink –
a slant, a glint, a cool spark
in the darkened room,

hears how light pings
a prism off the mirror's edge,
her glass of water tinkling
at its wink. She loves her dark
sonata, loves the music of the moon.

*How many different kinds of extreme music can you
imagine? The fantastical answers may turn out to say
a lot about a real place, or person.*

Extreme Aunt

My aunt Adelina... she went to extremes.

She climbed to her bedroom
  by the hard North Face, in winter,
    instead of the stairs.

She did things solo that the rest would do in teams.

She set off to school
  with her four huskies, *mush, mush!*
    to outrun the polar bears

She often woke up bruised from her dangerous dreams.

As a baby she would skydive,
  she would bungee in her harness
    out of her high chair.

My aunt Adelina... she went to extremes.

I remember her poised
  on the diving board, the top,
    with the wind in her hair.

She just had to go further, further and, it seems.

too far. We sent a deep sea diver

down into her bathtub
        till he ran out of air.

We used sonar, then we sent a submarine

but could we find her?
      No,
            not anywhere.

Extreme Uncle

Uncle Bradley was a moderate man
     but he took it to extremes.

He couldn't fall asleep without
     a riot of peaceful dreams.

Now, good sense is a noble thing
     but he overdid it badly.

        He made his mind up
    more or less,
       his No always
   halfway to Yes.
He took moderation to excess,
this patron saint of agreeableness,
        my uncle Bradley.

Uncle Bradley was a moderate man
     but he somehow couldn't stop.

Trying not to climb higher than anyone else
     he went right over the top.

Not going wild is wise indeed
     but he overdid it madly.

He bent over backwards
not to stand out,
      gave way at every
roundabout.
You only had to scream and shout
and he'd *give you the benefit of the doubt*
      (and gladly).

It had to end.
Faced with riot and rout,
      the whole world round the bend,
down the drain, up the spout
      that's when
he took command, he made a stand,
he took a deep breath and...   and...   and...

The time had come for Yes or No.
Then Bradley spoke. 'Well... I don't know...
    maybe...'
      Oh, uncle Bradley.

Tardigrade Takes a Selfie

Pan back
behind me. This
one is in black and white:
an island of bare granite in a hundred
howling miles of Arctic wind and snow and ice.

This one's
a bit dark: five
miles deep, me, in the black
sea-bed sludge, me, tucked in snug
by the weight of it, the Pacific Ocean on my back.

Here's me lit
by a volcano, in the seethe
and fizzle of a sulphur spring,
me on Everest, waving. But no, this is not
a holiday. This is my world. You're only visiting.

*

Tardigrade in the Cambrian Era

I was there from the off –
the sound of life revving up all over.
This was, oh, a cool half billion years ago.

Earth woke up from the ice
and yawned, its great continents breaking,
drifting. It stretched – okay, what now? –

as if a new sun shone. All round
the simple cells were mixing it, thrown
up and rattled, like God's crazy dice.

Yes, life whistling in the sunshine,
clanking its new toolkit – right, then,
what shall we build? what shall we be?

All kind of made-to-measure features:
shells? legs? eyes? Why
not? How many would you like?

I kept my head down, stepped aside
as this great armoured thing clanked past:
a trilobite. A clumsy model, but we knew,
                    we tardigrades: it wouldn't last.

Traces

300 million years, and what remains of us?
        A gap, but oh,
so accurately mapped: the track
of one soft body in the seabed mud,
one mouth, with one thought: *eat
        this? no, that?* reaching
                to and fro

until it imprinted a frill in the silt
        reaching as far
as hunger can. Or here's the burrow
where it hid from jaw-snap and claw-nip
to slip out its feathery drift-net.
        What we truly touch
                we are.

Or here at the end of a trail
        that tracery as fine
as your hair. It's a snapshot in stone
of panic. Even a death-throe
at this distance is a message, a Last Will
        and Testament,
                a signed

confession, a love letter even,
in copperplate script,
posted under the door and – no! –
      it slipped
under the door mat of stone

that we crack open now
and... Look, who's it
      addressed to?

             Do you really want to know?

Ichnologists: scientists who study traces like burrows or footprints left by living things, sometimes preserved in ancient rocks as fossils.

from Rooms With a View

A Tent~

> -ative place, a place in question, at a brink...

We've climbed, out of breath, out of daylight
till we pitched camp, by fumbling, by touch,
by the sound of our tent pegs — to sleep, to wake

to a new glow all round us... to blink:

what's out there? We hardly dare look.
Lift the tent flap slowly. It may be a dead drop,
a rattling scree, a sheer snowfield, or the edge

of a sulphur-breathed crater. Just think.

*

_If poetry was a building, what kind of building would it
be? Everybody has a different answer to this question.
So... what would yours be?_

Last Man Out

By night,
             one light
still burning on the soon-to-be-demolished
dim estate:
            the old guy
holed up in there, third floor,
      with the planked-up door,
            a haze
of smoky music through the cracked panes,

trailing vines
            and the cats
that come over the roofs in their dozens
to be fed,
            and parakeets
and yellow vervet monkeys,
       so it's said.
      But then again
they say that he's a poet. Who

knows if a word of this is true?

Freaks of Nature

A bird with three wings, that flaps in a circle,
known as Whirlybird or Helicopterus...
     A green snail with a solar panel on its shell...

A fish that lurks in deep sea shadow, tempting
travellers with the lantern on its nose...
     Believe me. I'm a poet. *Hmmm, well...*

A tea-fly that lives in the spouts of kettles
waiting for its dizzy mating flight,
     once-in-a-lifetime, in a cloud of steam...

A worm that eats its tail and lives for ever...
A safebreaker whelk that bores into the vaults of its prey
    with a diamond-tipped drill... *Huh. In your dreams!*

The acid worm that breeds in car batteries,
or in a lesser form, in pickle jars...
        Smart grass that simply lives on rain and sun...

A parasitic life form masquerading as a kitten
that propagates through its host's mobile phone...
    Oh really. Go on, pull the other one.

A giant creature who could overpower
anything, yet grazes on shrimps... A bird
 who's dentist to a hippopotamus...

A naked biped who looks up to space
and down through darkest ocean, and believes
 this whole colossal clockwork was wound up
 for us....

 That's it. You've gone too far now.
 That's ridiculous.

Beware! Six of these creatures are true. Four are not.
One is an ancient myth. One is an extremely modern joke.
Can you spot which is which?
If you'd like to check your answers go to p.96

Creatures, Great and Small

Homo sapiens, 'wise human'

Here's to you, the gallant caterpillar.
You go diving deep
into yourself, in the chrysalis,
dark as a bottomless sea.
Who knows if you'll come up again
(not you)
and if you do,
where, what or who will you be?

Here's to you, the faithful woodlouse.
You're all skin and bone,
poor squaddie in your body armour
marching day by day
into the damp, the dust, as things
break down.
All round,
the cities fall, the woods decay.

And Hom. Sap.?
Such a cheeky little chap
with a bric-a-brac brain and a feather in his cap,
his name's 'wise guy'.
He thinks he's home alone in this great big house
with the run of the place while the parents are out.
Sometimes he wakes up in the dark
and wants to cry.

Here's to you, the lithe and lissom slug.
        You mould your shape
to movement perfectly – half martial art,
        half ballet
in the horizontal. You move great
        and peaceful
        through puddle
and mud with the grace of a whale.

Here's to you, the philosopher spider.
        You cast out a line
as weightless as a thought
        and as strong,
then climb aboard, trusting the wind
        to carry you
        to a conclusion
which you'll have to live with, right or wrong.

And Hom. Sap.?
Such a cheeky little chap
(and chap-ess too, but we don't mention that)
        God knows he's tried.
He's got him a mission, he's got him a plan.
The name of the game is The Ascent Of Man
and he's going to keep going as fast as he can
        but something's rattling, loose,
                deep down inside.

Here's to you, mad mayfly, gambler.
        You stake everything
on one wild shuffle of the cards.
        You throw it all
up in the air: one shaft of light,
        one mating flight,
        one shake of the dice
and DNA, you don't care how they fall.

Here's to you, the alchemist earthworm.
        You take rot and dirt
and with a long slow *abracadabra!*
        you make soil as rich
as gold. (Oh, and your greatest trick
        of all: resembling
        the least of things,
half earth yourself, we can't tell which is which.)

> *And Hom. Sap.?*
> *Such a cheeky little chap*
> *though his past is a puzzle and his future's a*
> *Perhaps*
>   *he has his pride.*
> *The earth is his from Pole to Pole,*
> *the engine's revved and it's starting to roll*
> *but the whole thing is spinning out of control*
>   *and he's just the uppity ape*
>   *who hitched a ride.*

The species known as Homo Sapiens appeared around 2 million years ago, and is a close relative of great apes like gorillas and chimpanzees.

Modern humans appeared less than 200,000 years ago. An invasive species, Homo Sapiens now occupies almost every region of the earth.

Everything Is Relative

the ant's sudden yearning for a bit of me-time

the helter-skelter scurry of the sloth

the pigeon's puzzle: peck this seed or that one?

the ticklishness of the rhinoceros

the endless adolescence of the giant tortoise

the light bulb longing for a midnight moth

the blue whale overwhelmed by too much ocean

the crowded rush hour of the albatross

the hyena's sudden doubt:
                            what's there to laugh about?

            the patient panda getting slightly cross

the withering scorn
                    of the last rhino horn

                  for calculations of the profit and the loss

the human feeling that we've got it nicely sorted

            our strange conviction that we are the boss

Extreme Dining

That French restaurant, you know, with the fish tank
in the window – dim trout
that are yours for the picking? (Just point –
that one... Minutes later, it's cooked on your plate.)

Well, it merged with the bushmeat place next door:
Dundee's. Ostrich, kangaroo
and crocodile, of course – that's always
on the menu. Now it's Pick Your Own.

The whole garden's underwater, a mangrove swamp.
You pay your money, you get your canoe,
(in the shadows, dark ripples and a sluggish
splash...) your Swiss Army knife and harpoon.

Try not to notice: everybody's watching you
from the wide picture window upstairs –
the whole dining room
holding their breath with their forks in the air,

croc kebabs cooling on their skewers.
It's true
what the menu says: *Our food's so fresh*
it bites. Eat it before it eats you.

Bushmeat is the meat of wild animals in Africa, often
caught and sold illegally because the animals are in
danger of extinction.

Ways of Conquering Everest

... at all, the first time, ever
        ... by the direct route, in winter
... solo
        ... without oxygen or breathing apparatus
          ... travelling light

... all of the above, but barefoot
        ... without toes
... in secret, like under the bedclothes,
        with a torch, by night

... blindfold, trusting your guide
        extremely
... without maps, or GPS, or compass
        ... without a clue

... very politely, in the English fashion: *after
        you; no, after you*
... or if even that feels awkward, then
        forming an orderly queue

... the whole family, together
        (under 4s come free)
... in the amateur way: *did I climb that? Oh!*
        as if accidentally

... as a tourist, in appalling shorts,
      only here for the view
... in swimming costumes or
                 ... sky-streaking
      (very quickly, and completely nude)

... by mountain bike
           ... by yak
               ... by yeti
      ... by hook or by crook
            ... by the skin of your teeth

... by an enormous catapult, fired by a hundred sherpas
　　　　from the valley miles beneath

... in high heels
　　　　　　　　... in fun-furry slippers
　　　　... in princessy pink

... by extreme patience, with global warming,
　　　　without ice (and sooner than you think)

... piggy-back
　　　　　　　　... wheelbarrow-fashion
　　　　... as a three-legged race
... abseiling from a hot air balloon
　　　　... skydiving from the edge of space

... by none of the above,
　　　　I mean, let's not go to extremes
... when no one is looking,
　　　　not even yourself
　　　　　　　　　　... in your dreams

*With thanks to pupils of Hele School, Plympton, who gave
most of these ideas in a high-speed call-it-out session.
I just put them into shape.*

Worm's Eye View

Quiet up there
for a moment
please!

you lumberer

above ground,
flatfoot,
like a storm cloud full of stones...

slow thunderer

shaking the air
as if you could eat
the world with words, mouth always open,

you dull mumbler...

while *we* taste it whole,
the real thing: soil –
we take it in, till it becomes us. So

we under-

stand the earth.
It feeds us;
we feed everything that grows

and (here's the wonder

    of it) falls back.
        As you do.
Had you forgotten that, you know-

all, hungry
    plunderer?

        You feed the earth
eventually, you too.

Earthworms play a vital part in breaking down decaying matter by eating and digesting it, creating fertile soil in which plants can grow.

Tardigrade in Pyjamas

I'm all the fairy tales together.
I'm the bedtime story of all time.

The piglet princess
who became the crumbs
in the moss of the forest floor...

Are you yawning yet, you human
children? Sleep.
                    She dried her tears
and crept inside a bead of glass...

Lay down your heads. You'll never
go as deep
            as this... *And she hid*
in her castle of ice
and she slept for a hundred years.

*

Tardigrade in Space

out there
no air

no gravity
and a hundred degrees below

where you
can't be

except in a space suit as big as a fridge
I float free

look, I'm almost at home

in a dream
in which the stars

are whispering to me
saying... what? oh

wouldn't you just like to know?

*

Tardigrade in a Trance

I am no size
huge
in my world
in yours
small
one life
one life
for each
one life
for all

I have no name
no words
in my world
neither you
nor me
one life
one life
we all
swim through
one sea

I have no time
but now
a day
five hundred
million years

one life
one life
one always
now
one here

I am no one
not good
not bad
or any
thing
just am
one life
one life
one pulse
one note
time sings

oh yes, I have no ears – just know, in every cell: time sings

The Abyss

They say there are delicate shrimps

of no colour, like ghosts of themselves,
in ocean trenches past the reach of light,

as remote as deep space. They say there is smoke

that rises, black in the blackness, from rips
in the earth's core, through black water hot as fire

laced with acid and sulphur, like a Hell dissolving

upwards, water groaning with the weight
of ocean, three miles high. And the shrimp

with its feather-light gills, its pernickety feelers,

with its surgeon's kit of probes and pincers,
all its many pinpoint feet, goes tiptoe,

sifting, picking – it seems to be *dancing* its way

its way round the slopes of the crumbling
and shuddering drowned volcanoes,

a thing in a dream. You can't even think

what it's thinking, or knowing, or how,
except it comes to you: *Yes, me, here*

and whatever, I can live through this.

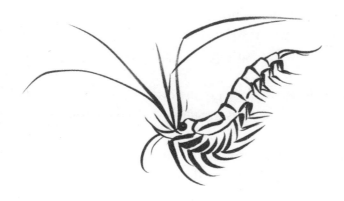

Singular

After the fiftieth insult –
the school bag down the toilet, the stifled
giggle-whisper that hung like a smear on the air –

she suddenly saw
there was another way to be:

the singular one,
who makes friends with the dark,
the cold, the weather no one else wants to go out in,

who makes it her own –
who won't accept a lift in hail and sleet,

who won't put up her hood,
who'll turn to face the slapping rain,
who's on a solo expedition, always, to the place

without maps, the place no one else
dares, and who survives it. See how almost casually

she walks straight through
the crowd (that stops its jostling
and goes still) as if she'd looked them in the eye

and said 'There's nothing
worse than this that you can do to me.'

Pioneers of the West

Through the 19th century, European settlers trekked across North America to claim and settle in what they believed was empty wilderness.
Native Americans had lived there, hunting the abundant wildlife, herding or farming, for at least 10,000 years.

You, clustered round your campfire, days beyond
the last name on the map,

you, circling your waggons into a stockade,

you, pushing the frontier back through sun glare
not even lizards choose to move in,

you, driving yourselves and dumb beasts to the edge

of nightfall – moonrise, low, so your long shadows
creep about and spook you... You,

trying to decipher it, that thin trickle of smoke

from one horizon, fading – pause – the silence
of the sky – before another answers,

you, who can't see what they say...

You of the West, did it ever occur to you
that this trail might go nowhere

or did you draw closer when that thought came

with your campfire songs, your hymns? All night
there were high looping howls

in the dark. They were telling you something,

the way mountains talk to each other, in the voice
of wolves. If even now you listened

would it be too late?

Whalefall and Boneflower and the Deep Sea Snow

Great whale, grey whale,
with the map of all the oceans
and their long songs in your brain,
    where do you go
at the end of all your singing?
    Weary one, oh

great, grave, gone whale,
who wove from that glittering string
a net so strong it held the sea's heave
    to and fro,
you were always the deep diver, deeper now
    than we can know

down and into the world beneath the world
    with *whalefall*
    and boneflower
    and the deep sea snow.

What falls as snow
a mile deep
is skin and scales

the food we eat
the food we are

one and the same
dropped crumbs
the body's waste

into the dark
forgetting

of ourselves
the flakes and cells
of life let go

to drift to fall

through stranger weather
than we can imagine

sleepless
dreamless
deep
sea
snow...

    Kind worms, blind worms
whom no one has seen or could love
how do you work, so dark, so cold
      a mile below
as delicate as seamstress fingers, to unpick
      the knot of bone?

Great bones, whale bones
that sank through blue green twilight
like an evening deepening forever
    slow on slow,
to lie like spars of galleons
    down where no

  light comes, and nothing
lives, except... *Osedax mucofloris,*
swaying like a pale bouquet of petals,
    the worm-flowers grow.

This is the world beneath the world.
where all life came from, maybe, maybe
    where we go,

    where we come home

      to *whalefall*
       and boneflower
       and the deep,
       the deep,
       the deep
       sea snow.

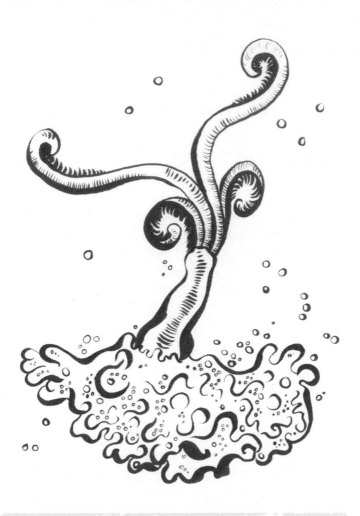

These worms help clean the deep sea bed by eating the sunken bones of whales. Anchored as if with roots, they look more like flowers than worms.
Marine snow is waste matter from all kinds of plants and animals that falls into the deep ocean, feeding the many creatures that live there.

Dark Sky Park

Now we're up on the edge
and over, on the mountain
with mountains beyond. Behind us,
     in the dark
of the valley, villages are embers
and the little city hugs its little glow,
ten miles away. Above,
     spark after spark
from a burned-out bonfire,
the stars spin away into space.
We huddle closer in our blankets, from the cold
     and the dark,
     in the dark
     of the dark sky park.

Tonight, look north, another edge
beyond this and... can you believe
your eyes – that blue-green fraying
     of the dark
of space, like fine weed wavering
in a stream? Where the solar wind itches
the thin skin of our atmosphere, the faintest
     watermark
of light – just breathe the word: *Aurora,*
Northern Lights – one that only appears,
and rarely, then, when held up

to the dark,
to the dark
of the dark sky park.

And us, where are we? On the edge
of the Earth. Are we riding this rock
bareback in the rodeo of stars? Or adrift
in the dark
in a small boat on the open seas
of space, thrown together, refugees
with nowhere to go back to or
to disembark?
Or picture this: a little boy out late
beyond the streetlights, dap-dapping his ball,
this one and only precious globe, alone
in the park,
in the dark,
the dark sky park.

*Most of us never see a really dark sky. Dark Sky Parks
are protected places far from the lights of cities where
we can truly see the stars.*
*The Aurora Borealis is a flickering glow in the sky
of the far North caused by particles of 'solar wind'
hitting the earth's magnetic field.*

About the Poet and the Illustrator

Philip Gross

is a multi-award-winning poet, writing for both children and adults. His 2009 collection *The Water Table* won the T.S. Eliot Prize, and his children's collection, *Off Road to Everywhere*, was awarded the Centre for Literacy in Primary Education Poetry Prize (the CLiPPA) in 2011. He is a keen collaborator with artists and musicians of all kinds. He has led writing workshops for more than thirty years – from 2004 to 2017 as Professor of Creative Writing at the University of South Wales – and has visited schools across the UK, working with teachers and young people. He lives in Penarth.

Jesse Hodgson

graduated in Illustration at UWE Bristol in 2012. Her first picture book *Pongo* was Highly Commended for the 2012 Macmillan Children's Book Prize and was published by Flying Eye Books in 2013. *Tiger Walk*, with Dianne Hofmeyr, is published by Otter-Barry Books in 2018.

Jesse created the illustrations for these poems with brush and ink. Her loose ink work style is also featured in the title sequence for the short film, Taniel, for Rebel Republic, which is premiered in 2018. Jesse lives in Bristol and draws from her studio on Spike Island.

TRUE OR FALSE? Answers from p.64
True: the angler fish; the whelk; grass; whale; the oxpecker bird that lives with hippos; the naked biped (us). The great worm or serpent Ouroburos comes from Egyptian or Greek mythology. The rest are made up (honestly), though why *are* there quite so many kittens on the Internet?